My First Picture Encyclopedia

Show Me
ROCKS AND MINERALS

by Patricia Wooster

Consultant:
Sandra F. Mather, PhD
Professor Emerita
Department of Geology and Astronomy
West Chester University

CAPSTONE PRESS
a capstone imprint

A+ Books are published by Capstone Press,
1710 Roe Crest Drive, North Mankato, Minnesota 56003.
www.capstonepub.com

Library of Congress Cataloging-in-Publication Data
Wooster, Patricia, author.
  Show me rocks and minerals : my first picture encyclopedia / by Patricia Wooster.
     pages cm. — (A+ books. My first picture encyclopedias)
  Summary: "Defines through text and photos core terms related to rocks and
minerals"— Provided by publisher.
  Audience: 4-8.
  Audience: K to grade 3.
  ISBN 978-1-4765-0116-1 (hardcover)
  ISBN 978-1-4765-3350-6 (paperback)
  ISBN 978-1-4765-3346-9 (paper over board)
  ISBN 978-1-4765-3354-4 (ebook PDF)
  1. Rocks—Encyclopedias, Juvenile. 2. Minerals—Encyclopedias, Juvenile. I. Title.
  QE432.2.W66 2014
  552.003—dc23   2013012354

Editorial Credits
Kristen Mohn, editor; Heidi Thompson, designer; Svetlana Zhurkin, media researcher;
Laura Manthe, production specialist

Photo Credits
Dreamstime: Maunger, 27 (bottom), Mopic, 27 (top), Nastya22, 10 (bottom right), Valariej, 28 (right); Getty Images: National
Geographic/Speleoresearch & Films/Carsten Peter, 10 (top); iStockphotos: Deborah Cheramie, 30 (left), Kim Gunkel, back
cover (middle), 4; NASA: JPL-Caltech/UCLA, 26 (left); Science Source: Joyce Photographics, 21 (bottom), Mark A. Schneider,
8 (bottom); Shutterstock: Aaron Rutten, 6, afitz, cover (bottom right), AGCuesta, 19 (middle), Alexey Bragin, 15 (top), Antoni
Halim, cover (top right), 1 (top), 20 (middle), AVprophoto, 9 (middle left), Balefire, 31 (bottom right), beboy, back cover
(bottom left), 5 (bottom), broukoid, cover (bottom middle), 29 (middle right), Christopher Boswell, 7 (bottom), dmitriyd, 9
(apatite), 24 (middle), 25 (top), Dmitry Pichugin, 29 (top), Dr. Ajay Kumar Singh, 23 (bottom), Dr. Morley Read, 23 (top),
eurobanks, 31 (middle), farbled, 9 (topaz), Frannyanne, 20 (top), fstockfoto, 17 (top), Gala_Kan, 9 (fluorite), Gavran333, 31
(bottom left), George Allen Penton, 29 (middle left), Ilizia, 9 (quartz), 11 (middle left), Imfoto, 9 (corundum), James Clarke,
30 (right), Jan Hofmann, 8 (middle), Jason Patrick Ross, 15 (bottom), Jiri Vaclavek, 23 (middle), kaband, 29 (bottom),
Karol Kozlowski, cover (back), back cover (back), 1 (bottom), kavring, 25 (bottom), Maciej Sojka, 26 (right), Madlen, cover
(bottom left), 24 (bottom left), Manamana, 9 (talc), Marcel Clemens, 9 (middle right), 9 (diamond), 17 (middle left), 27
(middle), Mark Higgins, 19 (bottom), Martin Lehmann, 18 (top), michal812, 9 (gypsum), 21 (top), NCG, 16 (top right),
Olga Miltsova, 5 (top), Only Fabrizio, 11 (top right), Photovolcanica, 14 (top), Rob Kemp, 17 (middle right), Robert
Crow, 14 (bottom), sa2324, 7 (top), Sergey Lavrentev, 9 (calcite), 11 (bottom), Siim Sepp, 16 (bottom), 17 (bottom),
slavapolo, 19 (top), Steven Gill, 24 (bottom right), Sumikophoto, 7 (middle right), Thomas Linss, 18 (bottom),
thoron, 13, Tom Grundy, 11 (middle right), Tyler Boyes, 9 (top and bottom, feldspar), 11 (top left), 15 (middle),
16 (top left), 20 (bottom), 21 (middle), 24 (top), 25 (middle), Vitaly Krivosheev, 7 (middle left), Yury Kosourov,
10 (bottom left), Zelenskaya, 22, Zigzag Mountain Art, 31 (top); USGS: Jeff Coe, 28 (left); Wikipedia:
CrankyScorpion, back cover (bottom right), 16 (middle)

Note to Parents, Teachers, and Librarians
My First Picture Encyclopedias provide an early introduction to reference materials for young
children. These accessible, visual encyclopedias support literacy development by building
subject-specific vocabularies and research skills. Stimulating format, inviting content, and
phonetic aids assist and encourage young readers.

Printed in the United States of America in North Mankato, Minnesota.
032013   007223CGF13

Table of Contents

Are You a Rock Hound?

Do you like rocks? Do you collect interesting rocks you find outside? If so, you're a rock hound! Each rock is different and tells a story about where it came from and how it formed. But what is a rock?

rock

nonliving material made from one or more minerals; some rocks contain materials that were once living; rocks are grouped by what is in them and how they were formed

Three Types of Rocks

- **igneous** rock formed when magma or lava cools and becomes a solid; may be formed either above or below ground; strong and mostly black, gray, or white in color
- **sedimentary** rock formed from sediment that builds up in layers; held together by the minerals silica, iron, or calcium; the layers can look like stripes; usually formed underwater
- **metamorphic** igneous, sedimentary, or other metamorphic rocks that have been changed by heat or pressure; can look glittery or striped with light and dark colors

4

geology

the study of Earth's history, rocks, minerals, soil, and other Earth features and how they are formed; also the study of features of other planets and moons

rock hound

a person who collects rocks

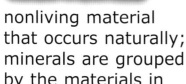

mineral

nonliving material that occurs naturally; minerals are grouped by the materials in them, such as carbon and aluminum

volcano

a landform created by an eruption when pressure builds inside Earth; many types of rocks are created from the heating and cooling of lava during this process; there are hundreds of volcanoes on Earth; some have huge eruptions, and others ooze lava slowly

Earth Is Made of Rocks

From the tops of mountains to the bottom of the ocean, Earth is built from rocks.

bedrock

a large solid piece of rock located below the soil, water, and loose materials such as sand; part of the crust

crust

the thin top layer of Earth that we walk on; it's up to 10 miles (16 kilometers) thick and made of many types of rocks including basalt and granite

mantle

a layer of Earth 1,800 miles (2,900 km) thick that is located beneath the crust; made of very hot, thick rock that slowly moves

core

extremely hot layer of Earth located beneath the mantle; temperatures there are as hot as the surface of the sun

sand

loose pieces of quartz or sandstone broken down by weather or water; the volcanic sands of Hawaii are loose pieces of weathered basalt; some beaches have sand that is broken pieces of seashells

sediment

tiny pieces of gravel, sand, mud, or limestone that have been moved by wind, water, ice, or gravity; can also be material from coal or coral reefs

canyon

steep cliff walls formed by water or ice cutting through them

mountain

a landform that rises above its surroundings; some mountains can be found on the ocean floor

Properties

Rocks are made from minerals. Sometimes you can find out which minerals are in a rock by observing the rock's physical properties. The next time you find a rock, see how many of these properties you can describe.

physical properties

the features you can see on a rock or mineral

color

the easiest property to see, but you usually can't tell what a mineral is just by its color

hardness

measurement of how easily a mineral can be scratched; talc, the softest mineral, is easily scratched; a diamond is the hardest mineral and cannot be scratched by any other mineral

streak

color from a mineral rubbed across a streak plate, which is made from ceramic; a spare piece of kitchen tile or your driveway can also be used as a streak plate; the color of the streak helps tell you what type of mineral it comes from

cleavage

how a rock or mineral breaks; some minerals break cleanly into sheets; minerals that do not break regularly have no cleavage

tenacity

how a mineral reacts to being crushed, bent, broken, or torn

luminescence

a glow some minerals give off under certain types of light, when heated, or when struck or crushed

luster

the shine of a mineral; it can be metallic (shiny), nonmetallic (dull), or waxy; gold and silver are shiny minerals

Mohs Scale

soft · hard

1	2	3	4	5	6	7	8	9	10
talc	gypsum	calcite	fluorite	apatite	feldspar	quartz	topaz	corundum	diamond

9

Minerals

Earth has thousands of minerals. But most rocks are made from the same few minerals. Here are some minerals commonly found in rocks.

crystals

When minerals experience a certain temperature and pressure, they form special shapes called crystals. Most rocks are made of a mixture of minerals with crystals of various shapes and sizes. Giant crystals in Mexico are as long as a school bus and as heavy as a blue whale!

feldspar

the most common mineral found in rocks; may be pink, gray, or white; used to make china, enamel, and glass

chlorite

green, yellow, white, or pink mineral; commonly found in clay

mica

(MIKE-ah)—silver to reddish brown mineral; found in granite and schist; used in paint, tires, makeup, rockets, missiles, and jet engines

hornblende

dark green to black mineral; found in many rocks including gabbro and basalt; used to make soap, oil, and statues

tremolite

white to gray mineral with needlelike crystals; commonly found in metamorphic rocks; used to make fire-resistant materials

quartz

mineral that comes in many colors; streak has no color; sandstone rocks contain lots of quartz; used in many things, including sandpaper, glass, and computer parts

calcite and dolomite

white and shiny mineral; stalactites and stalagmites in caves are made from calcite; used to make gum, glue, and toothpaste

The Rock Cycle

Rocks are constantly changing. They can be broken down and built back up. One type of rock becomes a different type of rock in the cycle. The cycle moves in every direction. This has happened to the rocks you see every day. Some rocks have taken millions of years to change form. And they will change again!

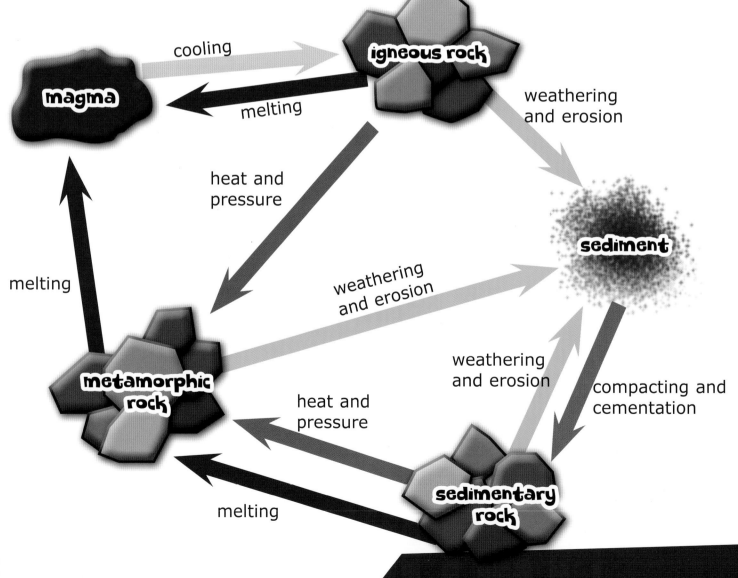

magma

cooling

igneous rock

melting

weathering and erosion

heat and pressure

melting

sediment

weathering and erosion

metamorphic rock

weathering and erosion

heat and pressure

compacting and cementation

melting

sedimentary rock

erosion

(i-ROH-zhuhn)—the process of moving weathered Earth material by wind, water, and ice

cementation

(see-men-TAY-shun)—when sediments become glued together by minerals or ice

weathering

rocks on Earth's surface are broken into smaller pieces because of wind, rain, ice, and hot and cold temperatures

pressure

(PRESH-ur)—weight of overlying rocks causing the rocks around them to change

compacting

weight pressing sediments together to create a rock

melting

a rock needs a lot of heat or pressure to melt; as a rock goes deeper into Earth's crust, the temperature gets hotter and the pressure gets greater

cooling

if a melted rock is brought back near the surface where pressure and temperature are lower, it hardens into a new rock

The Difference Between Magma and Lava

- **magma** molten rock and gases found below the surface of Earth
- **lava** molten rock that has come out onto the surface of Earth; the gases have escaped into the air

About Igneous Rocks

Igneous rocks form from molten magma deep inside Earth. When this magma cools, it becomes igneous rock.

felsic lava

thick and sticky lava that flows slowly; light-colored with minerals such as feldspar and quartz; it can form tall volcanoes

molten

melted

mafic lava

(MAY-fik)—lava that flows quickly and spreads over large areas; dark in color from dark minerals; some rocks formed by mafic lava are sharp-edged blocks and some are shaped like coiled snakes

solid

hard and firm; when magma cools it changes form and becomes solid

intrusive rocks

igneous rocks that formed from magma cooling below Earth's surface

extrusive rocks

igneous rocks that formed when lava extruded (pushed out) onto Earth's surface and cooled

Examples of Igneous Rocks

basalt

(buh-SALT)—a dark-colored volcanic rock formed from mafic lava; one of the most common rocks on Earth; 40,000 columns of basalt make up Giant's Causeway in Ireland

dolerite

a dark-colored speckled intrusive rock; used for building roads

gabbro

a dark rock with large crystals; gabbro is an intrusive rock; gabbro is made of the same minerals as basalt, but basalt is the extrusive form

granite

a hard rock with quartz and feldspar in it; cooled slowly and has crystals you can see; Mount Rushmore in South Dakota was carved from granite

obsidian

a sharp rock with a glassy surface; has the same minerals as granite but made from felsic lava that cooled very quickly and didn't have time to form large crystals; it is used to make surgery blades

pumice

(PUH-miss)—a light volcanic rock; looks like a sponge and floats on water; used in toothpaste, cement, and erasers

serpentinite

a beautiful green or red intrusive rock; the official state rock of California

17

About Sedimentary Rocks

The word sedimentary is related to the word "settle." These rocks form by various materials settling together to make rock. The materials might be plants, minerals, or shells of sea animals.

water action

moving water causing rocks and minerals to break down, become smaller, or to travel to a new location

glacier

(GLAY-shur)—a large piece of ice created by years of snowfall; some move very slowly at 1 inch (2.54 centimeters) a day, others move hundreds of feet in a day, and some don't move at all; glaciers compact and move sediment

strata

layers of sediment; scientists
study the strata to learn about
the environment at the time
each layer was created

porous

having spaces between pieces of
sediment; as layers are compacted
the pores become smaller

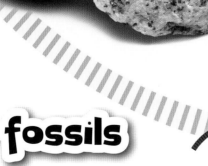

geodes

(JEE-odes)—a hollow rock with the
hollow space partly or completely
filled with mineral crystals; in Spain
a 26-foot (8-meter) geode was
found in a silver mine; geodes are
sometimes found in limestone

fossils

the traces of plants or
animals preserved in rocks;
found in sedimentary rocks

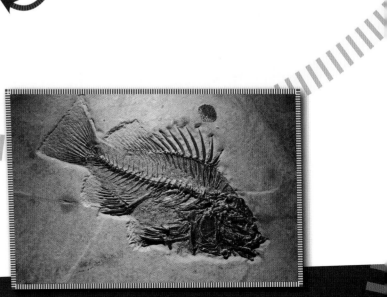

Examples of Sedimentary Rocks

chalk

pure white rock formed from calcite in the ocean; Mons Klint, a chalk cliff in the Baltic Sea, is more than 390 feet tall (119 m)

coal

formed when heat and pressure change plant material; the biggest source of energy creating electricity around the world

ironstone

a brown or gray rock found in shallow water; a source of iron

conquina

(koh-KEEN-uh)—a pale-colored rock made from shells of ocean animals

20

sandstone

made from quartz grains; some of the best dinosaur fossils have been found in sandstone beds

shale

made from mud and small particles called silt; natural gas is found in shale; fossils are often found in shale

mudstone

a rock of sticky clay and silt formed in quiet water; breaks into blocky pieces

About Metamorphic Rocks

Squeeze a tennis ball in your hand really hard. You are creating heat and pressure. This is what happens to all types of rocks when they change into metamorphic rocks. Some metamorphic rocks change into other metamorphic rocks.

metamorphose

to change into a different form; to have metamorphosis happen

heat

rock changes form in high temperatures

foliated

(FOH-lee-ay-ted)—having a layered or banded look caused by heat and pressure; nonfoliated metamorphic rocks do not have layers

fault

a break in a rock
where there has
been movement

dense

pressed tightly together;
metamorphic rocks are usually
more dense than the original
material they were formed from
because the material in them
has been compacted

agate

colorful minerals sometimes
found inside metamorphic rocks

joint

a break in a rock
where there has
been no movement;
caused by temperature
change, weight, and
salt growth

23

Examples of Metamorphic Rocks

gneiss

(NICE)—foliated rock with large grains in wavy dark and light bands

quartzite

metamorphosed sandstone

marble

metamorphosed limestone; white or gray, often with black, red, or green stripes; the Taj Mahal in India is made entirely of marble

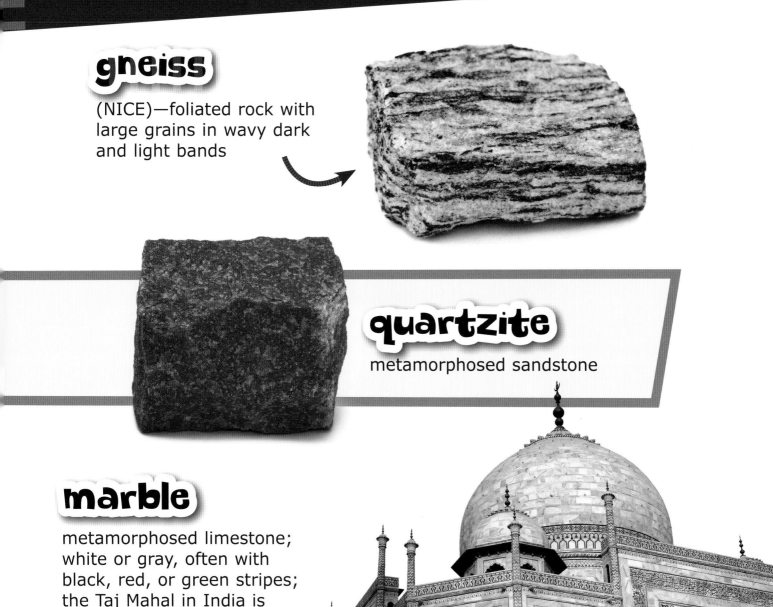

schist

foliated rock with medium grains in light and dark stripes; heat and pressure can change many types of rocks into schist

slate

metamorphosed shale

anthracite

metamorphosed coal; hard and shiny

25

Space Rocks

Rocks aren't just found on Earth. Billions of large and small rocks zoom through space. These space rocks help scientists learn about the beginnings of our solar system.

the sun and the eight planets, moons, asteroids, comets, and other bodies that orbit (go around) the sun

ball of dirty ice, rock, gas, and dust that orbits the sun; as a comet comes close to the sun, it sends off a long tail of ice and gas

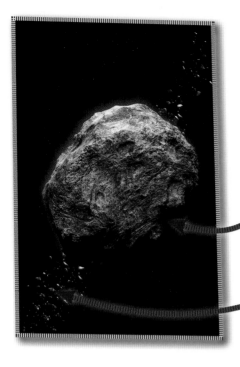

asteroid

odd-shaped rocky fragment left over from the formation of the solar system; some are as small as boulders, but others can be several hundred miles wide

asteroid belt

an area between the orbits of Mars and Jupiter where most asteroids are found

meteorite

a meteor that doesn't completely burn up in the atmosphere and lands on a planet

meteor

an asteroid that burns up upon entering a planet's atmosphere

crater

a large bowl-shaped hole in the surface of Earth or other planet, moon, or asteroid, caused by a meteorite crash; Earth's largest meteorite crater is in South Africa

Studying Rocks and Minerals

Rocks tell us much about Earth, its history, and natural resources. See how you can turn your love of rocks and minerals into a full-time job!

geologist

a scientist who studies the history of Earth and its features, especially its rocks and soil

petrologist

a scientist who studies Earth and its resources and searches for natural gas, oil, and underground water resources

volcanologist

a scientist who studies volcanoes and their effects on humans and other life on Earth

prospecting

searching for valuable minerals

gemologist

a person such as a jeweler or metal worker who works with gold, silver, and precious gems, such as diamonds

mining

removing minerals from Earth through open pits or from underground mines

Start Collecting!

You can find rocks everywhere. It's even more fun when you have the right tools. Start your collection today by rock hunting on the playground or at the park!

clean

it's important to wash the dirt off your new treasure; cotton swabs, tweezers, and rubbing alcohol are great for cleaning

identify

you can use a mineral chart, rock book, or the Mohs hardness scale to find the name of your rock

magnifying glass

take a closer look at your rocks and minerals with a lens that makes things look bigger; you can often see crystals in rocks when you use a magnifying glass

rock tumbling

using a device to wear the rough edges off rocks and polish them; many people like the smooth and shiny look of tumbled rocks

rock storage

you can store your collection in a sandwich bag, a plastic container, an egg carton, or a rock box that has special sections for each rock

goggles

always use protective eye gear when hammering rocks

rock hammer

a tool used to break open a rock to look at the inside

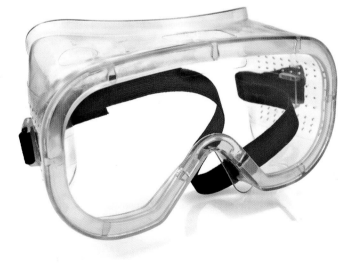

Read More

Pitts, Zachary. *The Pebble First Guide to Rocks and Minerals.* Pebble First Guides. Mankato, Minn.: Capstone Press, 2009.

Taylor-Butler, Christine. *Experiments with Rocks.* My Science Investigations. Chicago: Heinemann Library, 2012.

Tomacek, Steve. *Rocks and Minerals.* Jump into Science. Washington, D.C.: National Geographic Society, 2010.

Titles in this set:

Show Me
COMMUNITY HELPERS

Show Me
THE CONTINENTS

Show Me
DINOSAURS

Show Me
DOGS

Show Me
INSECTS

Show Me
POLAR ANIMALS

Show Me
REPTILES

Show Me
ROCKS AND MINERALS

Show Me
SPACE

Show Me
TRANSPORTATION

Show Me
THE UNITED STATES

Show Me
THE U.S. PRESIDENCY

Internet Sites

FactHound offers a safe, fun way to find Internet sites related to this book. All of the sites on FactHound have been researched by our staff.

Here's all you do:

Visit *www.facthound.com*

Type in this code: 9781476501161